Buddhism for Beginners

A Practical Guide to Spiritual Enlightenment

Copyright © 2015 by Tai Morello

Table of contents

Introduction

Spearheaded by leaders such as Jon Kabat-Zinn, mindfulness has been all the rage for many years now. Thanks to his Mindfulness-Based Stress Reduction (MBSR) program, mindfulness meditation has revolutionized the practice of clinical psychology. It is a key piece in the so-called "third wave" of cognitive and behavioral therapy. Inasmuch as it has triggered a paradigm shift in research and therapy, meditation is a *bona fide* big deal nowadays.

The influence of mindfulness meditation is not just limited to the field of psychology, however. Its influence has spread far beyond that area and into the self-help industry, corporate culture, education, and our daily lives.

At one time, meditation was only to be found inside the cloistered halls of Asian monasteries. That all changed with the rise of the 60s counterculture movement and with the small religious movements it left in its wake.

That paved the way for what meditation is today – a modern, cutting-edge, evidence-based, and most of all, *scientific* discipline. Far from just being a passing fad, it's beginning to transform our lives and our culture in a number of ways.

If you're wondering how the word *scientific* can possibly be applied to the discipline of sitting still, you're not alone. Thanks to fMRI scans and an increasing number of medical research by reputable institutions, it's now known that meditation is not just about sitting quietly with your legs crossed and your eyes closed. That's yoga, by the way, and though yoga does make use of meditation, such is not covered in the scope of this book.

From a medical standpoint, it is now understood that meditation has very real and very measurable effects on the human brain and body. Even more impressive, these effects can be repeated under controlled laboratory conditions.

According to the evidence so far, there are four parts of the human brain that seem to be the most impacted by meditation. As brain scanning technologies improve, however, we might actually discover far more areas that are impacted by this practice.

The first of these is the frontal lobe, which is the part of our brains directly behind our eyes. The frontal lobe is a major source of dopamine-sensitive neurons which are responsible for attention, motivation, planning, reward, short-term memory, and many other things.

Does the word "dopamine" ring a bell? There's a good chance that you have heard of its darker side thanks to drugs like cocaine, heroin, and nicotine. These substances boost the body's dopamine levels to cause that feeling commonly called a "high" among drug users.

Such highs cannot last, however, because the human body is not designed to withstand so much stimulation. This surge in dopamine levels must ultimately run out, causing what's known as a "crash."

Between stimulation and non-stimulation, as well as given a choice between pleasure and pain, people are geared for stimulation and will always choose pleasure. The unfortunate result, therefore, is the craving for more such highs in order to repeat the stimulation and experience more pleasure.

In other words, they crave more dopamine. This in turn can lead to drug addiction, and with it, all the anti-social behavior that goes with it. It is not the drug they're after, so much as the dopamine surge such drugs provide.

It is no accident, therefore, that a growing number of drug addicts and alcoholics who've tried and failed at other forms of rehabilitation are starting to turn to meditation. With the science backing it up, a number of health professionals, government sponsored health programs, and even private insurance companies have begun supporting such efforts – so far with promising, and cost saving, results.

The other part of the human brain that tends to light up the most on fMRI scans is the frontal lobe. This is considered to be the most "evolved" part of our brains because it is responsible for emotions, planning, reasoning, and self-awareness. Scans show that those who achieve deeper meditative states somehow shut down the functioning of their frontal lobes.

This does not mean they lose the ability to feel, to plan, to reason, or that they lose their sense of individuality. It only means that during deep meditative states, their brains seem to put these senses on hold – though why and for what reasons remain unknown as of this writing.

What is known is that the brain's tendency to shut down the frontal lobe seems to have an effect on practitioners even when their meditation sessions are over. The practical applications, if proven, are potentially staggering. Current studies are therefore ongoing regarding the use of meditation to treat post-traumatic stress syndrome (PTSD), childhood trauma, and other such psychological issues.

The parietal lobe also seems to slow down during meditation sessions. This can be found in the upper back part of our brains and is responsible for our sense of touch, pain, taste, and temperature, as well as language processing. Recently, it was also discovered that the parietal lobe governs our sense of time and space. It seems that during meditation, the human brain considers such senses irrelevant or unnecessary, and therefore, over-rides their functions.

There's also the thalamus, which can be found in the midbrain right above, and at the end of, the brain stem. Its function is to interpret all sensory data. Without the thalamus, we would have no way of processing anything we see, hear, touch, or taste. It is now known that this part of our brains regulates alertness, consciousness, and sleep. As with the parietal lobe, it also slows down significantly during meditation.

And finally, there's the brainstem, itself. This is surrounded by a set of interconnected nuclei called the reticular formation which go all the way down the spinal cord in three columns. Their functions are irrelevant to this topic except for the raphe nuclei which is where the production of a neurotransmitter called serotonin takes place.

Also called the "feel-good" hormone, serotonin has been found to increase the sense of well-being and happiness in both animals and humans. During deeper stages of meditation, fMRI scans have found that the raphe nuclei increases the amount of serotonin production for reasons that are still unclear.

While mindfulness and meditation are two completely separate disciplines, they are nevertheless inter-related for meditation requires mindfulness and mindfulness is an extension of meditation. At its absolute simplest, mindfulness is meditation in action – or as practitioners put it, "meditation when not sitting on the meditation mat." Both also have their basis in the same root – Buddhist teachings.

This book is not about finding a scientific basis for meditation and its effects, however. The research findings were presented merely to show that there is, indeed, some basis for all the hype. Unfortunately, much of it is hype because as more and more join the bandwagon, it is becoming harder and harder to separate evidence-based fact from wishful thinking fiction.

This has largely to do with a media that is far more concerned with profitable hype than it is with time-consuming fact-checking. Social media, spurred on by celebrities who rave about the benefits of meditation and mindfulness, as well as well-meaning friends and family members, also contribute to the hype.

This book is therefore meant for those who want to know what all the fuss is about, if anything. It is for anyone who is curious about the original source of all this mindfulness — that is, the philosophy and lifestyle of Buddhism.

This book does not seek to convert you to a religion. You do not have to sign a contract, join a group, or believe in anything.

Whether you're religious or secular, Christian, Muslim, or Jewish — or whatever — you can derive some practical benefit from the Buddha's teachings. The aim of this book, therefore, is to present Buddhism not as a religion, but as a *practical philosophy* for living with greater freedom and genuineness.

Chapter 1: Who was the Buddha?

The image on the left is a statue of the historical Siddhartha Gautama Buddha, known to Buddhists as the Shakyamuni – the Sage of the Shakya. The image on the right is Budai – a Chinese Buddhist monk who lived in 900 AD and is often confused in the West with the Shakyamuni Buddha. Although Budai is considered by Chinese Buddhists to be a Buddha because of his generosity and compassion, he is not to be confused with the Shakyamuni Buddha who founded Buddhism.

1. What the Historical Record Says

To understand Buddhism and its practical application in daily life, it is first necessary to understand its founder and his motivations. That he existed at all is not in doubt because of the historical record and archeological artifacts.

Based on these, it is believed that he was born in what is today the Village Development Committee of Tilaurakot in Nepal near the modern Indian border, sometime in either 563 BCE to 483 BCE. He then died sometime in 411 BCE or 400 BCE in Kushinagar within the Indian state of Uttar Pradesh.

His name was not the Buddha, however, for that is a title meaning either "the Awakened One" or the "Enlightened One." The name he was given at birth was Siddhartha Gautama. In Sanskrit, "Siddhartha" means "one who has accomplished a goal," while "Gautama" means "one who dispels darkness with bright light."

The exact details of his life remain both unknown and unverifiable, and even today, different Buddhist sects and communities have their own versions. The common thread that runs through them all, however, provides a precursor of his teachings and explains why he did what he did. It also explains why his teachings resonated with so many even within his lifetime.

2. The Official Story

According to the story, Siddhartha's parents were the king and queen of a kingdom. Before he was born, however, a sage had predicted that he would either be a great saint or a great warrior. Wanting him to be the latter, his parents ensured that he led a life of pleasure and excess, and did what they could to shield him from all unpleasantness. They went to such extremes, in fact, that those who had deformities or were ugly, as well as the sick, the infirm, and the dead were banned from the palace.

This couldn't last, however. Tired of his daily routine and his sheltered life, Siddhartha reached his boiling point at the age of 29. Wanting to see more of the kingdom he was meant to inherit, he snuck out of the palace with his faithful attendant. It was an eye-opener.

For it was only then that he encountered real life. The most shocking thing for him was seeing an old man, a sick one, and a dead body. Confused, he had to ask his attendant what those creatures were – for his parents had forbidden anyone to talk to him about sickness and death.

The attendant explained that all who lived must grow old, get sick, and eventually die. There was simply no escaping it. Siddhartha was already married, by then, and he had a young son. The thought of himself, of his wife, and of their child growing old, sickening, and eventually dying filled him with revulsion and he sank into a deep depression.

As he sat there trying to grasp the unvarnished truth, however, he saw a wandering ascetic pass by. The man, despite his old age, was filled with an inner peace that impressed the prince.

It was then that he made his first realization – that while old age, sickness, and death were unavoidable, suffering was another matter entirely. He therefore took leave of his family and relinquished his kingdom in order to find a way to end suffering.

3. The Middle Way

Impressed by his encounter with the wandering ascetic, Siddhartha took to the life of a wandering mendicant and sought out different spiritual teachers. They all taught him various disciplines, including yoga, as well as different forms of meditation. Though he mastered them all, he felt that they all lacked something and moved on.

His last teachers were extremists who taught him how to mortify the flesh. Their methods were too extreme, however, which nearly caused Siddhartha his life. Seeing how weak, sickly, and skeletal he'd become, he left his teachers and prepared to die.

That was when a village girl found him. Believing he was surely going to die, she gave him some food to ease his dying, but it did the opposite. Realizing that he was going to live, the girl and her family nursed him back to health, which was how Siddhartha received his second revelation.

On the one hand, an overly sheltered life of self-indulgent hedonism is a useless one because it leads to nowhere, accomplishes nothing, and serves no one. Worse, it makes one overly weak and overly dependent on external factors.

On the other hand, a life of extreme asceticism, one that denies the needs of the body, is equally unhealthy. Such not only harms the one who engages in it, but neither does it serve anyone or accomplish anything.

There had to be a healthy balance between the two extremes. This therefore became his guiding principle, which Buddhists call the Middle Way. It is likened to the tuning of a stringed instrument − if the string is too tight, it will break; but if it is too loose, it won't make a sound.

4. The Awakening

He therefore continued to study under different spiritual teachers, but was careful to avoid those that espoused extreme views or practices. Each time he mastered a particular concept or discipline, he was asked to take over for the master, but he always refused. Because though he learned something from each, he was never entirely satisfied and was convinced that there was still something missing.

One day, when he was 35-years-old, he sat down beneath a tree and vowed to meditate non-stop till he discovered the truth. After 49 straight days without taking a break, even for food, drink, and sleep, it finally came to him.

Excited, he wanted to explain his discovery to some of his former teachers, but discovered that they had passed away. In time, he made his way outside the Indian city of Varanasi and sat down to meditate. Passersby were impressed by the depth of his meditation, so when he finally came out of it, they asked him if he was a god.

He said "no." They then asked him if he was a messenger of a god, a holy being, or a prophet of some sort, but he said "no" to each. They then asked him what he was, to which he replied, "I am awake."

And that's how Siddhartha Gautama got the title of "Buddha" – the Awakened One

5. The Archetype

Whether or not the Buddha's story is true is completely and utterly irrelevant. Its appeal, especially to Buddhists, is the universality of his alleged experience.

Parents do their best to provide for their children and do what they can to shelter them from any and all unpleasantness. Even governments get involved by regulating the type of content that mass media can produce, banning foul language from being aired and providing ample warning in the event that adult content will be displayed – all to shield children from the harsher realities of life.

But such cannot last. Children eventually do grow up and want to stand on their own two feet – free from any parental guidance. The very content that government regulatory boards do their best to shield children from are the very things that young adults want to know about. They become resentful of parental guidance and control and want to experience life head on.

It doesn't take them long to realize that the world is not all about fairy tales with happy endings. There's poverty, there's sickness, there's tragedy, and there's death. For most, such things happen to someone else, not them. Until, that is, it actually does happen to them or to someone they know and love.

When the harsher realities of life finally stop being someone else's problem and become theirs, they cope as best they can.

Such coping mechanisms generally fall into several categories:

1) Escapism into drugs or alcohol – resulting in anti-social behavior,

2) Escapism into destructive behavior – such as violence or theft because they hurt and therefore want others to feel some of their pain,

3) Escapism into religion – which provides meaning for their pain and suffering,

4) Escapism into nihilism – the idea that life is meaningless or that all existence is a delusion as a way of either negating their feelings or in an attempt to disempower their feelings, and

5) Escapism into depression or insanity – since life is too much and their only way of coping is by surrendering to their feelings and shutting themselves off from the world.

These are only some of the negative coping mechanisms that victims of trauma engage in. More positive examples include:

1) Accepting suffering as a learning opportunity,
2) Accepting suffering as an opportunity for change,
3) Accepting suffering as a tool for introspection,
4) Accepting suffering as a means of growing stronger, and
5) Accepting suffering as inspiration for expression – artistic or otherwise.

In the Buddha's case, he did all of the above to one degree or another. His story, real or not, is therefore an archetype of:

1) How we originally grow up in an ideally sheltered environment,

2) How we eventually come to the understanding that life isn't always a bed of roses,

3) How we react to the reality of suffering, and the various coping mechanisms we use to deal with suffering, and finally,

4) How we move forward from such suffering, if at all.

6. Buddhist Philosophy has Practical Applications Today

What makes Buddhist philosophy so unique, however, is its approach to the idea of suffering, itself. The Buddha did not find a cure for all sickness, nor a cure for old age, nor a cure for death because none exists, whatsoever.

What he did discover was a way to understand suffering. By exploring various mental conditions that he tested and either rejected or accepted over a number of years, the Buddha found a way to get to the root causes of suffering in order to put an end to it.

According to his understanding, while the external world has things in it that can indeed be unpleasant (such as war, pestilence, and famine), they are not the actual causes of suffering, no. On the contrary, it is we, ourselves, who are the causes of our own suffering because of the nature of our own minds – which are inherently undisciplined. Such undisciplined minds create delusions which lead to preconditioned responses that in turn cause suffering.

Only by re-training our minds by observing its behavior can we undo our own preconditioned responses and thereby unravel our own delusions. Once achieved, we begin to understand the true nature of reality and live accordingly. Only in this state can we truly put an end to suffering – not in others, but within ourselves.

If this makes no sense, consider the case of war veterans who suffer from PTSD. Many continue to suffer even years after their tour of duty is over. It is not because the war followed them home, it is not because they are still being attacked in the safety of their own homes, it is not because their former enemies found them in their homes, it is because their minds still relive the horrors they endured. So though the battlefields they fought over may have known peace for years, in their minds, the battle continues to be fought.

Unable to endure such mental anguish, they seek therapy and take various drugs – both legal and otherwise. Despite this, it can take many years for them to ever get cured, if at all. The entire world may be at peace, their homes may be havens of safety, but their minds do not exist in the present. Their minds continue to dwell in a horrific past.

Though an extreme example, the Buddha would say that such is how the vast majority of us live our lives. We rarely exist in the here and now. Rather, we tend to exist in some mental bubble based on our experiences of the past or our hopes and fears of the future. So we live our days and nights physically present but mentally absent.

Living as we do with such mental blinders, how can we not but bump into things and therefore suffer? To put it in today's context, most of us think we're in control when we drive our cars. Unfortunately, many of us also like to text while driving – which has been proven to have disastrous results.

We can do nothing about the other cars, we can do nothing about the weather or road conditions, and we can do nothing about the traffic. But we can choose to put aside our cellphones while we drive or use hands-free devices if we insist on talking while driving. We can also choose to avoid texting while on the road.

This is what Buddhists mean when they refer to suffering and the causes of suffering. We can choose to live with mental blinders on (the causes of suffering) and end up regularly bumping into sharp objects (which is the experience of suffering). Or we can choose to remove our mental blinders and avoid bumping into sharp objects – like oncoming traffic.

Best of all, the Buddha didn't leave us with a vague set of instructions based on faith. One does not need faith to practice and apply Buddhist principles of meditation and mindful living. He left behind a complete system of detailed instructions for replicating his findings and reaping the rewards for ourselves.

13

He explained his new prescription for a nobly lived life in many ways, but the main ones we will explore in this book are divided into three parts:

- *Worldview* – which provides a framework for understanding the Buddhist path,

- *Lifestyle* – which prescribes an ethical way of living based on nonviolence and genuineness to ourselves and to others, and

- *Meditation* – which is the practice of calming your mind, refining your attention, and directing that powerful focus toward understanding your own mind from top to bottom. By doing so, you can then undo its neurotic patterns.

Chapter 2: Worldview

1. Suffering and Neurosis

Buddhism teaches that you must first have a basic understanding of what you're doing and why. Unless you can actually get down to the nitty gritty of your own intentions and motivations, neither meditation nor mindfulness will work for you because any kind of practice you do will lack direction and focus. You will start something only to stop it and change your mind, give up, start again, and so forth. You will have a lot of doubt and confusion about what you're doing, which will easily knock you off the path.

The reason for searching for a spiritual path (or some kind of therapeutic practice, if you prefer) in the first place is that we feel somehow dissatisfied with our current situation. We're restless and want to change something, so we go looking for solutions.

That may sound very general, but so is our sense of unease and dissatisfaction. This very general sense of unease is what Buddhism calls *dukkha*. This is not an easy word to translate into English, because like the word "love," it has a very generic meaning.

Dukkha originally referred to a sort of badly made wagon wheel – one where the hole in the middle through which the axle is fitted is off-center. Fit that to a wagon and drive off, and chances are that you'll get a bumpy and uncomfortable ride.
If you don't fix or replace that bad wheel, it'll eventually break and down you'll come tumbling to the ground. That's because something is off. The wheel is not well made. Its axle is off-center, so everything else will follow down an unpleasant path.

So the idea behind *dukkha* is that something is off in our minds. We're not crazy, necessarily, but we are looking at things sideways. We're off-center, and that creates the experience of suffering.

But *dukkha* does not mean "suffering" exclusively. Just as the word "love" in the English language can mean so many different things, ranging from a whole slew of different emotions to actions pertaining to the sex act, so *dukkha* is a flexible word. "Suffering" is the favorite translation of this ancient word, but *dukkha* can also mean unease, unhappiness, dissatisfaction, discomfort, and so forth.

Buddhist scriptures generally divide *dukkha* into three distinct categories:

1) Painful experiences, such as physical and mental suffering as a result of birth, aging, sickness, dying, and having things you do not want,

2) The pain you feel when things change or when you don't get what you want, and

3) The pain you feel due to a lack of satisfaction or because things and/or people fail to live up to your expectations

A more extensive list reads as follows:

1) Birth is *dukkha*, aging is *dukkha*, illness is *dukkha*, death is *dukkha*,

2) Sorrow, lamentation, pain, grief, and despair are *dukkha*,

3) Association with the unbeloved is *dukkha*; separation from the loved is *dukkha*,

4) Not getting what is wanted is *dukkha*.

For the sake of brevity and unless otherwise specified, we'll use "suffering" from here on out when translating *dukkha*.

The Buddha took it yet a step further by claiming that the attempt to avoid suffering leads to suffering. So instead of running away from it, one must confront it armed with his insight. For he discovered that the nature of suffering is that our experience of suffering has a cause. The cause of suffering is form of neurosis, which consists of passion, aggression, and confusion.

- *Passion* is the way our minds go after some object, person, or experience that we desire. Passion is what impels us to act in order to get those things, it moves us to action, often without thinking of the consequences. There's a sense that we want to draw that object, person, or experience into our territory, to possess them, and to make them part of our little treasure hoard — especially if they make us feel good. Whether that object, person, or experience will actually make us feel good is irrelevant, at the time. All that matters is that we give in to our passion and act accordingly until we possess those things. So rather than let things naturally be, we try to draw them into the sphere of our control. We want to make them *ours*.

- *Aggression* is passion's opposite, or more like its evil twin. Whatever is unpleasant or makes us feel bad, we want to throw up a defensive wall to stop it; we want to launch an attack on it and destroy it. The instinct here is the same as in passion. We have our little territory, which we think of as *mine,* and we want to make sure nothing threatening can breach it. If it has already made its way past our defenses, we want to destroy it.

- *Confusion* means that we are insensitive and indifferent to the way things work. We don't notice how cause and effect work; we have no clue that when this happens, that happens, and we never learn from our mistakes — or, for that matter, figure out how to reproduce our successes. So we keep doing the things that, in the long run, make us unhappy, and we're too confused to do the things that will bring us happiness. We could also call this stupidity or cluelessness.

These three neuroses work together to produce the experience of *dukkha.* To understand how that is, it helps to explore the different kinds of suffering in greater depth. Put another way, we can divide *dukkha* up into three different contexts: plain old suffering, suffering as a result of change, and background suffering.

- The *dukkha* of suffering is any suffering of the obvious sort. You step barefoot on a piece of broken glass. Your boyfriend or girlfriend leaves you, which breaks your heart. You have to spend long hours on a tedious task at work, leaving you bored and restless. A stranger insults you, which makes you feel angry. You catch a cold.

  Obviously, practicing Buddhism isn't going to remove the pain of a foot injury or alleviate the discomfort of a bad cough. But what it can do is to transform the way you experience and respond to the many knocks and bumps and irritations of life. When we try to maintain ourselves and protect and/or enlarge our little territory, we just compound our suffering. Take that out of the picture, and pain becomes simple, direct, and manageable.

- The *dukkha* of change means that one minute we're happy, and the next we're not. Because everything is constantly changing, we find it hard to hold on to anything. We cannot secure a cozy situation for ourselves, because situations always tend to fall apart. So you might enjoy a well-paying, steady job for years, but one day the company faces budget problems and you get laid off. Or you're enjoying an ice cream, but the scoop of ice cream falls out of the cone and lands in the dirt. Even before the situation changes, the *dukkha* of change is already there, as a potential. Somewhere in the back of your mind, you know that things can't keep going so well forever.

- The *dukkha* of conditionality, or background suffering, is always present. It means that because whatever experience you have is colored by passion, aggression, and confusion, it already contains some subtle level of suffering in it — always. This suffering is pervasive and subtle and lurks in the background. It is a nagging sense of anxiety that leads you to try to maintain and protect yourself and your territory, to create a little island of immunity in the confusing and threatening flux of life.

2. Further complications

Once we're already stuck in the pattern of churning out neurotic states of mind, the process has a way of keeping itself going in perpetual motion. One of the Buddha's key insights, which was revolutionary at the time, is that mental states are like anything else: they come about due to causes and conditions. A seed planted in the ground, when it meets with the right conditions of water, sunlight, and good soil, first sprouts and then grows into a fully sized plant.

Likewise, the life of the mind — the inner world of our experience — also follows a regular pattern of cause and effect, something that Buddhism calls *dependent arising*. When you set up the right conditions for *dukhha*, then you will have the experience of *dukkha*. And when you set up the right conditions for eliminating that suffering and experiencing freedom, you will have the experience of freedom from *dukkha*.

The Buddhist understanding of dependent arising is that the first event in this process causes a cascade of events that leads to the last one, and the last one then feeds back into the first one. This then keeps things going in a cycle. This feedback loop just reinforces itself again and again, generating more and more distress and suffering. So the idea is to stop the feedback loop. Somehow or another, we have to remove the causes and conditions that keep the loop going.

The first link in this chain is fundamental *ignorance*. This means that at the root of our problem is a mistaken thought or belief, a lack of the right kind of knowledge. Specifically, we don't have the knowledge of impermanence and non-self (more on this later), which are the basic nature of reality. Because we get the basics so wrong, we get just about everything else wrong, as well. So ignorance is the true origin of our distress.

Ignorance lays the foundation for our *mental conditioning*, which is the way our minds are predisposed to certain kinds of thinking, and as a result, certain kinds of action. Some people are predisposed to certain bad habits — smoking, for example. They are already *conditioned* to act that way. They are conditioned by their environment, by their own previous actions, and by their ignorance about the basic nature of things.

So, to continue this example, if we understand the nature of impermanence, then we'll know that the pleasure that comes from smoking is fleeting, that it puts us at risk for certain kinds of illnesses, and hastens the approach of death. If we understand non-self, we won't be disposed to self-identities that reinforce this habit of *I am a smoker, I smoke because X, Y, and Z,* and so on. Conditioning includes everything from this simple example to full-blown psychological complexes.

Ignorance and conditioning are mostly subconscious. We're not really aware of them most of the time, but there they are anyway, influencing everything we think, say, and do. They provide the condition and background for *consciousness*, which is the next link on the chain. Here, when Buddhism talks about consciousness, it doesn't mean a passive awareness of the world. This consciousness has a forward momentum and projects you into new situations, always pushing you into new kinds of action.

The way Buddhism thinks about things is a little different. Our usual idea is that we have a body and a mind, and that consciousness is an operation of that mind. But the Buddhist way of thinking always puts *experience* front and center. So, because our experience of consciousness is very basic, it is considered to be the foundation of our experience of *body and mind*. Any knowledge we have of our bodies, or of having this or that mental state, comes through our conscious experience of being a human in a body, our conscious experience of having a mind with all its thoughts, emotions, etc.

From this experience of body-and-mind comes our *sensory* experience. Consciousness moves forward, into the experience of body-and-mind, and then out towards the world, which it perceives in terms of sight, sound, smell, taste, and touch. Let's add another sense: consciousness. It is also aware of an inner world of thoughts and emotions, a mental sense.

The world "out there" comes into *contact* with the senses. And from our point of view, this contact is either pleasant, unpleasant, or neutral — that is, it has a *feeling* to it. Now, whether an experience is pleasant or unpleasant is highly individual and based on each person's conditioning. Many people are fond of cucumbers, while others simply cannot stand them.

Based on that pleasant or unpleasant feeling tone of an experience, another link in the chain comes up: *tanha*, which can be understood as thirst. The word "thirst" is a bit misleading here, because it refers not just to wanting things, but also to wanting to get rid of some other things. From that perspective, really wanting to get a massage is a *thirst*, as is being annoyed by the mosquito which bit you and feeling an intense thirst to get rid of it. An alternative to the word thirst in this context, therefore, would be craving.

The mind first craves, then it reaches or *grasps*. Because we crave something so badly, we try to grasp it, and stick to it like meat to a hot frying pan. So, with craving, we have a desire, while with grasping, we act on that desire.

Here, if we're good meditators, we have an opportunity to introduce a break in the feedback loop. A kind of space occurs between craving and grasping, a split-second gap in the chain of events. With a disciplined mind, it's possible to open that gap and stop the chain of events before they reach grasping. You have to be ready for it, because once you're grasping, it's already too late.

Grasping just fuels the fire and leads to further developments. Because we took action, our situation changes, grows, expands. This movement toward new states of being, fueled by the action of grasping, is called *becoming*, and becoming leads to the maturation of new situations and states of being, called *birth*.

Here, birth doesn't specifically refer to the literal act of being born from the womb or giving birth to a child. Birth, in this sense, refers to a new set of desires which sets forth a new cycle of sensing, craving, grasping, and becoming.

Say you want a house, for example. That's the birth of a new desire. That desire, in truth, has little to do with the house, itself. It comes from your desire to have a sheltered place to hopefully keep you safe. This is only natural, as we have physical needs which help sustain our existence.

Because of our cultural conditioning and other factors, however, a simple shelter that keeps us warm in winter, cool in summer, and safe from whatever elements nature decides to throw at us is not enough. We want a house that's beautiful, but even that isn't enough. Ideally, we want a house that's bigger than what our neighbors have because we feel that such will earn us respect and admiration.

What respect and admiration have to do with shelter is completely irrelevant, but that's how the mind works. There is no such thing as a desire that stands on its own. All desires are inter-dependent. Give in to one desire, and you find yourself in a maze that branches off into other desires which, though completely unrelated to your original desire in the logical sense, makes complete sense in the emotional neurosis of your mind.

So you get a house that's bigger than what your neighbors have, but now you have to fill it with furniture – hopefully of the type that's nicer and classier than what your neighbors have. That's a new thirst, right there. Assuming you get that, you'll want a car that's nicer than what everyone else has, so there's a new thirst right there which leads to yet a new cycle of sensing, craving, grasping, and becoming.

As you engage in ever new cycles of wanting and achieving, only to end up wanting and achieving even more, you forget the catch. That you have to pay for it all with compound interest on your credit card. This leads to worry and stress. So to make up for it, you have to work harder and take out more loans, leading to yet more worry and stress. What should have been the simple fulfilment of a valid need – the acquisition of a house to shelter you from the elements – has become a source of worry and stress.

The end result is that you now have a new thing to thirst over – the desire to be free of debt, free of worry, and free of stress. And so a new cycle of sensing, craving, grasping, and becoming gives birth to yet another set of desires. The feedback loop continues on and on and on.

But because of impermanence, whatever is born has to die and whatever begins has to end. Any new situation we experience will start to fall apart and finally expire. This last stage is called *aging and death*. It is the true fruit of ignorance. Decay and death cause us tremendous suffering *because* of our ignorance of impermanence and non-self. We try to freeze or solidify our ever-changing experience, including our experience of self. We would like to believe that, underlying all this change, is a solid, consistent, unitary "*I*" that remains the same — in other words, a *self*. This habit is a deep feature of our psychology, and, as we'll see, it causes us a lot of grief.

We forget that who we are today is not the same person we were years ago. Can you remember what you were like and how you thought as a child? Chances are that you can't. Can you remember what you were like and how you thought as an infant? Very unlikely. So there is no continuity of "I-ness" between you as an infant and you as you are now. Nor is there a continuity of your "I-ness" when you are unconscious or asleep.

There are whole gaps in your memory that amount to years, and yet you still believe that your sense of who and what you are is unbroken and whole. You acknowledge that you have grown up, have matured, and are still learning. While true, there is no such thing as a continuous "I-ness."

You therefore exist under the delusion that a continuous and unending chain of being, of awareness, and of identity has existed between the moment you were born and the person who is now reading these words. Despite the fact that your chain of consciousness, your sense of "I-ness," is broken every night when you fall asleep, you still fear death because you fear that it is the end of your sense of self – even though your sense of self dies every night.

3. Impermanence and the conditioned nature of things

We've already talked about impermanence a bit, and we've talked about the idea that whatever we experience comes about because of dependent arising. The life of our minds, the world of our experience, is not random or senseless, but orderly and intelligible. Not only that, but these experiences, though very personal, come about due to causes and conditions.

The Buddha had some deep insights into dependent arising. Whatever comes into being from a cause, he called a *conditioned thing*, and any conditioned thing, he said, is impermanent. That is, if it has a beginning — if it can come into existence — then it is subject to change and will have an end, also. That goes for people as well as things. It goes for the mind, the body — everything.

This means many things. It means any pleasure that we have will not last. Friendships turn sour or slowly fade away. Marriages fall apart. Bank accounts empty out. Fortunes are made and lost. Good health lasts only for a time.

It also means that we will die in the literal sense that our bodies cease to function, something we don't like to think about. But in the Buddhist way of thinking, it's very important. Buddhism is about living well, and if we live well, we will die well, also. Buddhism puts importance on living and dying nobly and gracefully, with genuineness and dignity. Someone who has lived well will not struggle when they die, but will pass away with a peaceful heart free from regret.

We don't know the hour or cause of our death. It could come soon or late. It could come suddenly or gradually. So we don't really know how much time we have. If you consider this again and again, you'll have a keen awareness of your own mortality and won't waste any time. It will be easy to prioritize what matters in life and what does not. With a fire burning under your butt, you'll get straight to the important matters of life without delay.

In the early days of Buddhism in Tibet, there was a group of hardcore monks called the Kadampas. They kept their monastic vows very purely and lived simple, disciplined lives. Every night when they went to sleep, they wouldn't cover the embers of their fire so as to rekindle it the next day, but would just let the embers go cold. If they died in the night, they thought, there would be no need to rekindle the fire, so what was the point?

These Kadampas would turn their alms bowls upside down when they went to bed. The reason for this is that in Tibetan culture, a dead person's cup and bowl would be left overturned. By overturning their bowls when they slept, these Kadampa masters reminded themselves that each time they lay down to sleep, they might not wake up again.

Even today in India, bodies are cremated. Since it takes at least six hours to turn a human body into ash, these crematoriums are considered to be unclean places because corpses have to be stored there until their turn at the fire comes. Those are the lucky ones. Unfortunately, many Indians, then and now, are poor.

Funerary rites in India and Nepal have always been very expensive. Not only do the mourners have to pay for the priests and funerary attendants, but they also have to pay for the firewood. A typical funeral pyre in India requires between 1,102–1,323 pounds of wood to properly dispose of a corpse – representing a tremendous investment on the part of mourners.

Since not all can afford the expense, most resort to a type of ritual burning – that is, bodies are burned for show. When the wood runs out, the burned corpse is dumped into a river, if available. Otherwise, wild animals are allowed to enter the cremation grounds and eat the remains once they've cooled. This process continues to this day and was certainly so during the Buddha's day. As such, entering cremation grounds is considered a polluting act, one that requires ritual purification after the funeral rites are over.

The Buddha, however, saw a valuable learning opportunity in such open air crematoriums. So rather than avoid them, he spent time in them and instructed his disciples to do the same.

He told them to observe bodies as they advanced through the different stages of decomposition which are described in gruesome detail in various Buddhist scriptures.

The point of such an exercise had nothing to do with a morbid fascination with corpses. The point was to really drive home to his disciples that they, too, would one day die and that their bodies would also fall apart to be eaten by crows, vultures, dogs, and worms. The other point of this exercise was to teach them the inherent delusion behind lust. Even the youngest and most beautiful body was nothing more than a corpse that had yet to give up its ghost.

In other words, a Buddhist practitioner should constantly keep two ideas in mind. The first is that powerful emotions, like lust, are fleeting. Not only do they pass, but the thing which inspires such powerful feelings are temporary. The most beautiful woman or gorgeous man is nothing more than a sack of meat that will one day feed maggots; the most beautiful architecture will one day be nothing more than a bleak ruin; and the most up-to-date sports car will one day be nothing but ugly metal turning to rust in some scrap heap.

The second thing to keep in mind is the impending reality of death. Just as nothing lasts, so no one lives forever. Time is a limited, and therefore, precious commodity which should never be wasted or taken for granted.

The crematorium therefore served as a final reminder of why it was so important to study and practice Buddhist principles in order to alleviate suffering. Those who waited till they suffered unbearably before actually putting Buddhist teachings to use were those who had waited too late. This is exemplified in the Parable of the Burning House.

One day, a wealthy man went home and discovered that it was engulfed in flames. To his even greater horror, his children were inside. They were so busy playing with their expensive toys, so distracted by their fun, that they didn't notice the flames coming closer and closer to them.

The terrified father screamed and pleaded at them to come out before it was too late, but the children didn't understand why he was so upset. They were far too engrossed in their games so they told him they'd come out when they were good and ready to, and not a moment sooner.

The father replied that he had brought them newer and better toys. But if they wanted to have them, they first had to run out of the house as quickly as possible or he'd give them to someone else, instead. Shrieking with excitement and delight, the children poured out of the burning house and were surprised at what they saw waiting for them outside – it was a cart filled with precious stones and pulled by a white bullock.

The father in this parable is the Buddha, of course, while the bullock cart and jewels represents Buddhist teachings. By sending his disciples to the gruesome open air crematoriums of India and Nepal, the Buddha was hoping they'd truly understand the peril they were in and act accordingly.

Nowadays most of us won't get a chance to observe the decomposition of a human body in real time. But we can practice awareness of impermanence, all the same. Whenever you sit down to meditate, take a minute or two to think about this life. You don't know how long or short it will be. Each year that goes by subtracts that much time from your life; each day brings death closer. Death draws nearer with each passing moment.

As you go about your day, keep impermanence in the back of your mind. When you enter a building, think that you might not exit it again. When you say goodbye to a friend, consider that you may never get a chance to say hello to them again. Tell yourself that each day, each hour, each minute might be your last. With each action, think to yourself, "This might be the last thing I ever do."

German theologian Georg Hermes put it best when he said that, "Death is an arrow already in flight, and your life lasts only for as long as it takes to reach you."

I don't want to make you very anxious about death. But you should come to value your time so highly that you don't waste any of it. Your time in this life is limited, but you don't know how limited. So make use of it while you have it. Use it to become the person you want to be rather than just following the same old habits robotically. Make good use of your life while you still have the chance.

4. What is non-self?

One of the more popular religious ideas that was making the rounds in the Buddha's time was that of the *atman*, meaning the eternal *Self*. According to this idea, every person has an ultimate Self. This is what we ultimately mean by the word *"I,"* which is a single thing, one with the eternal Absolute, and not subject to death or decay. Liberation, they thought, would be achieved when the changing nature of body and mind, and all the lesser desires of the lower ego, were purified and fell away, and one experienced the pure, eternal light of the Self.

The Buddha explicitly repudiated this idea and thought that any philosophical speculation about the Self — its existence or nonexistence — was a useless way to spend one's time. Instead, he encouraged practitioners to look at the body and mind in meditation, to look at the many goings-on — sensations, feelings, thoughts, emotions — and examine them, asking, *Is it permanent or impermanent? Does it last forever, or does it come to an end? Is it independent, or does it come about because of a cause? Is it singular or multiple? Is it me, mine, I, my Self?*

Before we proceed further, let's just stop and consider this process of examination for a minute. What this process is is an investigation into a fundamental belief that we all have by default. Nowadays, in the twenty-first century, most of us don't believe in the idea of an eternal, independently existing *atman* – at least not as specified in the exact doctrine of the *Upanishads*. These are a body of Indian philosophical literature which sought to distance themselves from the heavy ritualism of Vedic Hinduism.

To the writers of the *Upanishads*, true sacrifice wasn't about buying expensive items only to burn them on a pyre in the hopes of gaining something from the gods. True sacrifice was about sacrificing one's ignorance and preconceived notions. Only then, they believed, could one begin to understand the true nature of reality and be free from the delusions of the world.

Those *Upanishadic* philosophers suggested that the *Self* was more than just a spirit that survived the body's death. They believed that it was something far greater, so much so, in fact, that it was equal to the Supreme Being:

> He (the atman) *who is in the fire, and He who is here in the heart, and He who is yonder in the sun – He is one*
> (Maitri Upanishad 6.17)

But the teaching on non-self is not just about the philosophical *atman*. It is about the intuitive belief we have that each of us is an "I," that "I" am a single being, a self, and that while my body and mind are constantly going through changes, there is something unchanging that endures beneath all those experiences, and that it therefore possesses these experiences.

So this intuitive belief is about what we could call the *self* or the *ego*. It is this "I" that remains within us and that defines us, despite the fact that we are not who we were as children, and despite the fact that we lose consciousness when we sleep.

The Buddha, however, disagreed and proposed the concept of *an* (Sanskrit for no, not, none, without) *atman*. *Anatman*, therefore literally means "no self." He challenges our commonsense notion of who and what we are, and says: That notion that you have an inherent and unchanging self is false, an error. He takes it a step further by claiming that such commonsense, intuitive grasping at a self is the very reason we experience *dukkha*. It is this fundamental ignorance that we need to cure if we're to be free from *dukkha*.

This is a bold and outrageous idea, even today, but not unique in India. Long before the Buddha's time, there was a school of thought known as the Charvaka. The Charvaka School descended from the Lokayata and Brihaspatya schools which emphasized the value of philosophical skepticism. More specifically, they were atheists who disdained religion and religious ritualism. Charkava rejected gods, an afterlife, prayer, and karma, claiming that:

> *There is no other world other than this;*
> *There is no heaven and no hell;*
> *The realm of Shiva* (the Hindu god of destruction) *and like regions, are invented by stupid imposters.*
> (Sarvasiddhanta Samgraha, Verse 8)

It is clear from his own discourses that the Buddha spent time with the Charvakas and was greatly influenced by their empiricism. Charvaka taught that all knowledge could be gained from either inferential or deductive reasoning using the physical senses, through trial and error, and by looking for exceptions to a condition. Yet even when one has come to a conclusion, one must be skeptical for two reasons.

The first is that our senses are flawed and we cannot help but feel an emotional attachment to preconceived notions. The second is to make room for new knowledge, or at least, to suspend judgment till an exception to a claim has been found. Above all, however, the Charvaka rejected any explanation which referred to the supernatural. The Charvaka, in other words, were India's early pioneers of not just atheism, but of the scientific method.

This approach of philosophical skepticism can be found not only in the Theravada branch of Buddhism (more on this later), but in the Jain religion, as well. The latter is not surprising since Jainism's founder (the sage Mahavira) also spent time with the Charvakas and was a contemporary of the Buddha. This explains the many similarities between Jainism and Theravada Buddhism, though whether or not the two men ever met is unclear (despite many legends that say they did).

31

The Buddha, however, had by then become wary of extremes. Just as he found hedonism and extreme asceticism to be both unhealthy for the mind and body, so he found extreme religiosity and rabid atheism unhealthy for the mind. While he, himself, did not believe in a god, neither did he deny the existence of one. When confronted with the age-old question of "Does god exist?" he was actually cagey in his responses.

When asked what they should therefore believe in, the Buddha said:

Do not believe in things simply because they have been repeated often,
nor because they are based upon tradition,
nor because they have been rumored,
nor because they are found in a scripture,
nor because they have been based upon surmise,
nor because they are based upon an axiom,
nor because they are based upon specious reasoning,
nor because they are based upon a bias towards a notion that has been pondered over,
nor because the one who says so seems competent and able,
nor upon the consideration that, "This monk is our teacher."
Kalamas (the people he was speaking to), *when you yourselves know:*
    "These things are good; these things are not blamable;
    these things are praised by the wise; undertaken and
    observed, these things lead to benefit and happiness,"
    Believe in this and abide in them.

(Kalama Sutta)

This skeptical and rigorous scrutiny of information was not to be reserved only for rumors, sayings, scriptures, or culturally accepted "facts," however. Such a skeptical scrutiny is also to be applied to one's mind. The Buddha therefore taught that if you looked at all the parts that make up your own experiences and searched for evidence of a self, you wouldn't find any no matter how hard you tried. The self, he concluded, is just an empty concept that we cling to because the alternative — that there is no *I*, not really — freaks us out.

To help his students investigate this idea for themselves, the Buddha divided up all the constituent parts of a person into five categories or aggregates. He could have divided it up into three, or four, or six, or any other number, but he chose five. So while the number may be arbitrary, it's still very convenient, because it gives us a framework for examining ourselves.

The five aggregates are:

1) Form (or body),
2) Feeling,
3) Perception,
4) Conditioning, and
5) Consciousness.

These categories include every part that makes up a person, body and mind. The idea is that, if you go through them one by one looking for the self, you will not find it. And if you keep looking, and keep not finding it, you will grind the intuitive belief in the Self down further and further until, in the end, you have a direct, experiential realization of non-self.

To get some idea of what non-self means practically, think about your own situation. Start by considering your body. At the moment of conception, you were only a single cell in your mother's womb. You don't even remember that. Could that single cell really have been *you*? And at what point did you become "you?" Was it when the embryo developed into a fetus? Was it the moment of your birth?

You don't remember your birth, either. You were just a helpless, crying bundle of arms and limbs. You can trace a line back in time, connecting the person who's reading this book right now with that crying baby — but is it you? Is there really a Self there?

The body is constantly changing, constantly in flux. Cells are constantly being replaced with new ones. In seven years' time, not a single cell in your current body will still be there. Is there any abiding self in the body, or is it just a constantly changing phenomenon?

Then consider your own thoughts and feelings — your mind. Chances are, your mind is constantly changing. It is even more in flux than your body. Memories provide some feeling of continuity, but that also is deceptive. Psychologists have found that memory is very tricky, subjective, and not very accurate. So memories can't be relied on to provide a continuity of self.

Consider how much has changed from when you were born until now — your childhood, your adolescence, all the years in between. We like to construct a story out of all this where we are the central character. But much of our lives has a random, disconnected quality. It's a stream of events going by and we're trying to put it together into some coherent narrative.

Perhaps it's only by convention and force of habit that you call that person ten years earlier your "me," and you assume that ten years down the line, whoever "you" are will still be you. It seems very likely that your idea of *I, myself* is put together from various pieces that are all made to fit together.

So where does your sense of self reside? If there are vast gaps in your memory, if the things you believe in now are not what you used to believe in before, if your personality and attitudes are not the same as you were as a child or as a baby, then where is the "you" that believes there is some form of continuity?

Since your body's cells replace themselves every seven years, it can't be in your body. What you sense is based on faulty sense organs, which in turn provide an inaccurate view of the world around you. Take your vision, for example. If you believe in it, objects shrink the further away from you they get and railroad tracks eventually meet up somewhere in the distance. Since your senses are faulty, then your perceptions must likewise be faulty. Taking that a step further, does it not also mean that your "sense" of who "you" are is likewise faulty?

Conditioning is the result of cultural constructs. Your parents, your teachers, your classmates, friends, mass media, and your government have conditioned you to think, to believe, and to react to stimuli in a certain way. They have taught you that you are the citizen of a particular country, that your obligations are such and such, that you must feel good about certain things and bad about others. Industry has taught you that you must buy by getting into debt because the economy will always be a certain way.

In America, they used to think that slavery was good. Fortunately, that country no longer believes in such things. Up until recently, we were all encouraged to invest in real estate because all the experts told us that real estate values always go up. Yet the world still hasn't entirely recovered from the Global Economic Crisis that advice brought on. Since cultural beliefs, and therefore, cultural conditioning continuously changes and evolves, your sense of "I-ness" cannot possibly rest on your conditioned responses.

Which brings us to consciousness. If your consciousness does not reside in your body, or your senses, or your perceptions, or your conditioning, then where does it reside? In your brain? But your brain is a physical organ and we've already covered that bit. In your mind? Where is your mind?

The Buddha asks us to ask ourselves these questions. Who is the person reading this now? You see these words with your eyes, perhaps you touch the pages of this book (or the computer screen you're reading these words on) with your fingers. But who is the one reading? Who is the consciousness processing the information, animating your eyes, and controlling your fingers? Where does it reside? Can you point to your head or any other part of your body and say, "It is here!" If so, where?

We will talk about this a bit more in the meditation chapter, but for now it's enough to understand what non-self means and how it fits into the big picture.

5. Breaking the feedback loop

A further audacious idea of Buddhism is that freedom from self-created suffering is a true possibility. Suffering is a conditioned thing, and like all conditioned things, impermanent. So remove its conditions, and it will come undone.

This is not just held up as an empty promise to try to seduce people into adopting a new set of beliefs. You can actually get a preview of this freedom through the practice of meditation. It is actually possible, by sitting down and getting to know your own mind, for you to catch a glimpse of what lies beyond the veil of confusion.

The Buddha did not say much about this state of freedom, at least not in positive terms. It seems he was concerned that people would try to turn it into an eternal substance, or grasp it as a self. But he did connect it to what he called the "luminous mind." According to him, the mind, unfettered by neuroses created by self-inflicted suffering and delusion, has a natural radiance about it, or a clear, luminous, and knowing quality.

But this natural luminosity is obscured by the buildup of habitual thought patterns that dull and cover its original radiance. So you could say that the Buddhist path is about wearing down this buildup, rubbing and polishing it again and again to remove every last speck. It is like a mirror that has been covered by centuries of dirt and grime. The mirror can be cleaned, and once it is, it can shine brightly, once again. But it will take a lot of patient and careful work.

* * *

If you've made it this far, you're doing well. The "Worldview" chapter is in some ways the most difficult chapter in this book. It's difficult because it's a little abstract and hard to understand. But everything we've covered in this chapter is very important for grasping the context of the next two chapters on lifestyle and meditation. So if you put in a little more effort toward understanding the theory behind all this, it will pay rich dividends later when the rubber meets the road of practical engagement in ethics and meditation practice.

Chapter 3: Lifestyle

What's missing from much of the modern mindfulness movement and craze for meditation is a strong system of *ethics*. There's a sense that morality — the principles of right and wrong that guide our actions — is just an afterthought. This is a mistake. The Buddhist take on morality is that it gives us a context for walking the spiritual path. Or as one Buddhist teacher put it, morality "sets the atmosphere."

So it's worthwhile to look at your own behavior closely and decide if it's really in line with your deepest principles. And if it isn't, then that's an area you need to work on.

The Buddhist idea of morality is that we can be moral without being moralistic. Living a good life, being a good person, doesn't have to be about a big finger wagging in your face and telling you you've been a bad boy or girl. Instead, it's about a process of becoming more and more who you really are – which is a being inherently filled with love and kindness. It's about being direct and genuine with yourself and others.

Morality in the Buddhist sense is an expression of your willingness to give up your ego and its complicated games so you can be kind and noble towards others – not because you want something in return, or because it's the right thing to do, no. It's because acting that way is your true nature.

The Buddhist idea of morality is based on the principle of *ahimsa*, non-harm or non-violence. This is the same *ahimsa* that was the guiding principle of Gandhi's political revolution for Indian independence, which in turn inspired Dr. King's non-violent activism during the Civil Rights Movement to end racial segregation in the United States.

In Buddhism, living a moral life is about not harming yourself or others in thought, in word, and in deed. When we intentionally do something to harm ourselves or others, we are under the influence of neurosis: passion, aggression, or confusion. We might steal from someone because we're greedy for their possessions. Or we might hit someone, or even kill them, out of anger and hatred. We might even hurt ourselves because of some deep seated guilt or pain, or worse, kill ourselves because of the same.

If we're under the spell of ego-clinging, we're so caught up in our perception of *my* rights and *my* needs, *my* desires and *my* injuries. We can be so caught up in how we were insulted and slighted, that we can just as easily ignore the rights and needs of others. But each of those others is just like us. Each of them contains within themselves a whole world of hopes and fears, dreams, thoughts, feelings, and so on. Each of them wants to be happy and avoid suffering. *Right morality*, as the Buddha called it, is about respecting this fact and refraining from any action that will harm others and ourselves.

The questions we must therefore ask are:

1) How do we avoid causing harm – either to ourselves or to others?
2) How do we live in an ethical way?

3) How do we live in the world with all its ugliness and find a way to be kind and genuine – not only to ourselves but to others?
4) And how does doing any of the above help to alleviate our own suffering?

According to the Buddha, the answer lies in the Eightfold Path. The Buddha did not invent this path, but took it from far older traditions taught to him by his various teachers. According to him, it was by following it that he achieved the self-understanding which led him to his awakening – his Buddhahood. The symbol of Buddhism is therefore a wheel with eight spokes, each of which represents the Eightfold Path.

Though presented in a list form, it is not to be understood in the same way as the Ten Commandments of Judaism and Christianity. The different aspects of the Eightfold Path are to be understood as the different parts of a single whole and should therefore be practiced accordingly.

Their order does not, in any way, indicate their importance as each is considered to be of equal value. Each one supports and reinforces the other, like the separate fingers of the hand. Although we have names for each of our fingers, as well as for parts of the hand like the palm and the back of the palm, we refer to the entirety as the hand. The Eightfold Path must be seen in the same way.

Thoughts lead to words which lead to actions. So if you allow yourself to hate, for example, you might direct that hatred toward someone else. Once you give in to that feeling, you might vent by saying hateful words toward that person. The next step is to engage in hateful action by physically hurting that person.

The Eightfold Path proposes getting to the root of the matter, (your hatred, in this example) and fixing it before it gets to the stage where someone gets hurt. In order to do that, each aspect of the Eightfold Path is divided into three distinct sections:

I. Wisdom
  1) Right View
  2) Right Intention
II. Ethical Conduct
  3) Right Speech
  4) Right Action
  5) Right Livelihood
III. Concentration
  6) Right Effort
  7) Right Mindfulness
  8) Right Concentration

If morality indeed sets the atmosphere for mindfulness and meditation, as that Buddhist teacher so rightly put it, then wisdom is the foundation on which that morality is built. Without wisdom, morality becomes whatever anyone says it is. Without wisdom, morality changes and adapts to different times in order to suit different needs and tastes. Wisdom may therefore be thought of as the constitution which provides the guiding principles upon which we can base our actions.

And so we come to Ethical Conduct. Conduct is about acting, because morality without action has no value. Preaching and praising morality but not actually practicing morality is gross hypocrisy. It becomes nothing more than a philosophical construct that has no practical application. Ethical conduct is therefore needed.

It can be argued that all religions and all moral philosophers have said the exact same thing at all times and in all places. What makes the Eightfold Path different, therefore, is that it describes the meditative exercises and practices which tie it all together. So Wisdom is the foundation for Ethical Conduct, Ethical Conduct is Wisdom in action, while Concentration is what keeps the whole thing going and takes it to the final level where *dukkha* ends.

1. Right View

The Kalama Sutta just about sums up what the Buddha meant by Right View. He taught people to use their critical judgment not just toward everything they see, hear, and are taught, but toward their own thoughts and feelings, as well. We are raised with so much emotional and cultural baggage that we're not even aware of them. Despite scientific discoveries proving that all humans everywhere are pretty much the same, for example, racism still persists with often disastrous consequences. Despite the fact that women have proven themselves just as capable as men in all professions and fields, sexism still persists with equally tragic results.

In his *Apology*, Plato wrote that, "An unexamined life is not worth living." The Buddha couldn't have agreed more. Right View means understanding that you are not your nationality, culture, political ideology, others' expectations, nor what you think you want out of your life. If you define yourself in that way, then you will always be other than what you truly are. As such, you become a victim of both yourself and others, as well as ever-changing circumstances.

As you question yourself, your thoughts, your feelings and motivations, however, there should be one guiding principle by which you should live your life until you get to the bottom of who and what you really are – harm none, including yourself.

2. Right Intention

They say that the road to hell is paved with good intentions. Such is, indeed, often the case, but that is only so because there's a vast difference between good intentions and Right Intention.

The Buddha explained that there are three conditions which fulfill the criteria of Right Intention:

1) The intention of renunciation,
2) The intention of goodwill, and
3) The intention of harmlessness.

He further explained that there are three conditions which negate Right Intention:

1) The intention governed by desire,
2) The intention governed by ill will, and
3) The intention governed by harmfulness.

Each of the first three negates and therefore counteracts the second set. The Intention of Renunciation means wanting to do good without any thought of reward. Mundane Right Intention was what the Buddha called the latter, which he defined as doing something in the hope of getting something out of it.

Although Mundane Right Intention isn't necessarily bad, it still carries the taint of wanting some benefit. In sales, this is what's called *What's In It For Me?* or WIFM. Help me, please. *Why, what's in it for me?* Do good. *Why, what's in it for me?* Feed the poor. *Why, what's in it for me?* Help the sick. *Why, what's in it for me?* Stop doing that. *Why, what's in it for me?* When we renounce any thought of WIFM, we counteract Intention Governed by Desire.

Sometimes, even the best Mundane Right Intention is governed by desire. We want to help the drug addict into recovery, we want to help the battered housewife get to a women's shelter, and so on. Our intentions may be genuinely good, but addiction is a complex phenomenon, as is the psychology of those who remain in abusive relationships.

The sad fact is that if people are not psychologically or emotionally ready to receive help, they'll refuse it. Attachment to the idea of a favorable outcome for that drug addict or battered housewife is still a desire, one that sets up yet another paving stone on the path to hell. And this is why we see burned out social workers, frazzled emergency dispatch operators, and manic depressive guidance counselors. Their intentions were genuinely good, but their actions were governed by a deeply-seated desire for a favorable outcome.

If they could have but held on to their Intention of Goodwill while letting go of their Intention with Desire, they could offer their help with equanimity. Their goodwill remains for any and all who want and need their help. But they neither oppose those who refuse it nor force it upon those who aren't ready. In this way, they maintain their Intention of Goodwill – also called Loving Kindness. There's no sense of, "Oh *now* you want my help!?" Their goodwill is such that it's always there, waiting for the other to overcome their blindness and pain till they're good and ready for help.

3. Right speech

The Buddha counseled others to engage in speech that is "factual, true, beneficial, endearing, and agreeable to others, with a sense of the proper time for speaking." This was to be done not out of a sense of propriety, but rather out of a compassion for others. He urged his followers to reflect before they speak:

> *"This verbal act I want to perform — would it lead to self-affliction, to the affliction of others, or to both? Is it an unskillful verbal act, with painful consequences, painful results?"*

If so, then it is best to avoid it. In other words, avoid lying, abusive, and divisive statements, as well as useless gossip.

As an experiment, without trying to change anything, just observe yourself when you lie or twist the truth, or speak harshly or abusively to someone. How do you feel? What kind of effect does it have on your mind? Check yourself carefully for about a week.

After that, take another week, but this time, carefully avoid saying anything dishonest, equivocating, verbally abusive, or insulting. When you speak, speak with kindness, gentleness, and honesty. Then check how you feel. Look carefully at your mind.

My prediction is that you'll feel lighter, happier, and more confident by the end of week two. That's because you're being honest with yourself and others, and giving up the games you play with your words — which are actually like a huge burden you don't even realize you're carrying.

4. Right action

This is an extension of Right Speech – if words can hurt or heal, then so can actions. At its simplest, Right Action means not to harm or kill anyone, including animals. This doesn't mean you have to become a vegetarian. Though if you are inclined to stop eating meat because you feel compassion for animals, that would definitely be a good thing. It would be enough, however, to just avoid inflicting any physical or psychological harm on people or animals.

Included in this category is to refrain from stealing. Stealing is usually motivated by desire or greed, and Buddhism defines it as taking what's not given. Stealing depletes the wealth and resources of others. It's not a small thing. People work hard for money. They put a lot of energy into making it, so a lot of energy also goes into the things that they own.

If you've ever been a victim of theft, you know that it can create a good deal of hardship, pain, and frustration. So instead of enriching yourself by taking from others, it is much better to put in your own honest effort and earn money legally. Nor is stealing simply about robbing someone with a weapon or taking something away from them when they aren't looking. Stealing includes taking things by stealth and by deceit.

The next point is to refrain from sexual misconduct. Buddhism is not trying to get into the bedroom and tell consenting adults what they are and are not allowed to do. But irresponsible sexual behavior can be very destructive and cause a lot of disturbance in people's lives. Half an hour of pleasure has the potential to cause tremendous chaos and pain. So it's best to avoid sleeping with people who are married or in a relationship. Likewise, more obviously harmful kinds of sexual misconduct like rape, sexual assault, and sex with minors are definitely off the menu.

Here, as elsewhere in Buddhism, the guiding principle is non-harm. It's not that sex is dirty. But it is, as you yourself may have experienced, unpredictable and fraught with all kinds of strong emotions. For someone training their mind to become more peaceful and free from emotional turmoil, Buddhism advises them to carry out their sex lives with thoughtfulness and sensitivity to others. So it's not a matter of no sex. It's a matter of thinking through the potential consequences before jumping into it.

The Buddha also advised his followers to avoid the use of intoxicants which lead to mindlessness. He was not against alcohol and drugs, per se. What he opposed were their effects on the mind. Those under the influence of mind-altering substances, including alcohol, are incapable of being mindful. Under the best of conditions, such people become harmless. Under the worst, however, they can become abusive or careless, as is the case with drunk drivers who harm or kill others unintentionally.

Since it is mindlessness that leads to suffering for both one's self and others, it becomes even clearer why the Buddha didn't have a high opinion of intoxicants. He also saw them as instruments of escapism – yet another cause of suffering.

What it boils down to is living carefully, or for the purposes of this book, *carefulness*. Carefulness is the application of mindfulness in the arena of social life. Acting carelessly, we may think that we're being very spontaneous and authentic, but we're actually becoming slaves of ego-clinging and the neurotic mind. When we act carefully, we bring presence of mind into every situation. We live a life in accord with our deepest principles, a life we can be proud of. And we "set the atmosphere" for creating a healthy, light, and spacious mental environment for ourselves.

This has an influence on our minds, making us more relaxed and peaceful. Others can sense this, too. They want to be around us, because we are respectful and pleasant. Our sense of peace and wellbeing rubs off on them, and they also benefit from it. So being careful with our behavior is a way of being compassionate to ourselves and others, something that's hard to do when we're tipsy, drunk, or stoned.

5. Right livelihood

Finally, something needs to be said about Right Livelihood. How we earn a living, putting food on the table and money in the bank, is not an afterthought. It is of utmost importance to a life well lived. Occupations that harm others, such as those that deprive them of wealth, for example, slaughtering animals, or pumping harmful chemicals into the environment, not only spread chaos and pain, they also diminish our own integrity.

In the Anguttara Nikaya III. 208, it specifically states that one must not trade in weapons, living beings, meat, alcoholic drinks or those that lead to a loss of mindfulness, as well as poison. While some would argue that this is a difficult thing to do in this day and age, what it boils down to is a matter of choice and personal responsibility.

The Buddha could not possibly have predicted the myriad of complex professions that now exist, but he did understand that there are certain professions that cause harm. What the fifth path asks people to do is to consider the potential consequences of how and what they do for a living. Does someone who works at a weapons factory bear some responsibility if those weapons are used to commit genocide, for example?

Most today would say "no." They would argue that if Company A didn't produce weapons, then Company B and C would, and the average Joe needs to put food on his family's table. The fifth path would counter with the question of: "Then what would happen if Joe's family were the victims of the very weapons he made?"

This is obviously a very complex topic and continues to be debated within Buddhist communities today. Since the fifth path asks people to consider the potential consequences of how they earn a living, it also raises the question of gray areas. A devout Buddhist obviously cannot work as a bartender or a cocktail waitress. But can they be the carpenter who builds the cocktail lounge or the janitor who cleans it? Or the farmer who sells grain to the brewery that turns it into beer?

Many therefore argue that any work which is honest and legal, that does not knowingly, willingly, or actively seek to cause suffering or harm, constitutes Right Livelihood. As such, working as an assassin, a torturer, a soldier, or a toxic waste dumper constitutes wrong livelihood because one cannot possibly take up such professions without knowing full well what is expected of them.

What it boils down to is the need to make a living in a responsible and ethical way. And if it's possible to earn a living in a way that directly helps and benefits others — like a career in social work or medicine — then that's even better. That way, our spiritual path is not just our own individual trip, but is an active, social engagement that improves society for everyone.

This is best exemplified in the story of a monk who wanted to practice morality. He had the courage to look at every single one of his actions honestly and decide if it was good or bad. Every night before going to bed, he would take out a collection of stones, half of which were black and half of which were white. He would then go over his actions for the day.

If he did something kind, honest, genuine, noble, or generous, he would place a white stone in one pile. If he did something unkind, selfish, rough, harsh, violent, dishonest, manipulative, without integrity, or was stingy, he would put a black stone in another pile.

At first, the pile of black stones was very big, while there were only one or two stones in the white pile. But as he carried out this exercise day after day, thinking carefully about how he carried himself and conducted himself each day, the black pile started to shrink and the white pile grew. In the end, he had only a large pile of white stones at the end of each day.

He noticed changes in himself, as a result. His mood was always light and carefree. His mind was free of stress and worry. He carried a heart of happiness with him everywhere he went. He spoke only words that were gentle, true, and meaningful. People instinctively liked and trusted him because they noticed his genuine goodness. You can also follow this monk's example and experience the results for yourself.

Here's another exercise: Consider what will happen in your life if you give your worst traits and habits free reign over you. What would become of you if you just let yourself go, let your worst side take over? Imagine the disaster you would make of your life. Write it down. Don't spare any details and don't be afraid to make a fully grim prediction of how bad things could get.

Now consider whatever good qualities you have and whatever good qualities you wish to have. Imagine the kind of life you will have if you always live out those good qualities instead of the bad ones. Write that down also, again imagining it as vividly as you can.

Now imagine the kind of future you want for yourself. What kind of person do you really want to be? What will people think of that person? What kind of friends will that person have? What company will that person keep? What behavior does that person show? Again, be specific. Imagine your best future self vividly and write it down. Consider the moral qualities of your best future self. Which virtues do you have? How did your future self get to be that person? What moral qualities did you cultivate? Write it all down, then again and again strive to become that person.

Being truly kind means being kind to whoever you will become in the future, also. If you practice goodness and genuineness now, then that person in the future will have happiness. So think about what kind of life you are creating for that future "you"— whoever that is.

Chapter 4: Meditation

At last we come around to what you've been waiting for, meditation. Without meditation, there is no Buddhist path. It's what makes the whole journey workable from beginning to end. It is the method *par excellence* of training yourself and working with your mind.

But what is meditation, exactly? The word itself conjures images of blissed-out yogis on mountaintops intoning *Om* and tripping on their spiritual good vibes. That's not entirely inaccurate, but it's a little silly and stereotyped.

The Sanskrit and Pali word for meditation is the same: *bhavana*, which means "cultivating," "development," or "producing." In Tibetan, it's *gom*, which has a sense of "getting used to" or "familiarizing." That's important because the idea of meditation can be intimidating if we don't have any experience with it. We may think we can't do it because we can't sit still long enough, empty our minds, or concentrate.

The good news is you don't have to worry about that. Meditation is a process of development and cultivation. It's a process of *getting used to* your mind and yourself, of getting used to the meditation technique. And as long as you're actually sitting on the cushion and looking at your mind, you're doing all right.

You may think you're already used to your mind and yourself, but chances are, if you're like most people, you're not. We live busy lives. We have many activities and responsibilities, and full schedules. So most of us don't actually take the time to sit on our butts and get to know ourselves. If we do find ourselves with a few quiet minutes alone, we might feel uncomfortable and restless. We quickly reach for the remote, or turn the magazine page, or check Facebook. Sound familiar? We go to great lengths to avoid being alone with our minds.

But, as boring or even painful as it may feel at first, spending some time alone with your mind and getting to know yourself is one of the kindest things you can do for yourself. Yes, it is painful sometimes to see what kinds of thoughts we really have in our heads, to shine a light on our hidden corners. But before meditation, our minds are like an old storeroom that hasn't been cleaned for decades, but just keeps gathering junk. Meditation opens the doors and windows wide open, clears out the dust and cobwebs, lets in the fresh air and light of day. It is tremendously refreshing. It makes us feel lighter, more relaxed, and more spacious.

And so we come to the last three items on the Eightfold Path – those which fall under Concentration.

Buddhist scripture is very clear about what this entails:

Here the monk arouses his will, puts forth effort, generates energy, exerts his mind, and strives to prevent the arising of evil and unwholesome mental states that have not yet arisen.

He arouses his will... and strives to eliminate evil and unwholesome mental states that have already arisen.

He arouses his will... and strives to generate wholesome mental states that have yet to arise.

He arouses his will... and strives to maintain wholesome mental states to keep them free of delusion, to develop, increase, cultivate, and perfect them.

(Sacca-Vibhanga Sutta)

Right Resolve is called a *sankalpa* – a vow to make a determined effort to see something through to the end. It isn't enough to say you'll do something. Nor is putting in the effort enough. In business, signing a contract obligates you to fulfill that contract to the best of your abilities. A company's ability to fulfill contracts is a reflection of its success, while one that frequently fails to see a contract through is one that doesn't last very long and goes bust. Right Effort/Resolve therefore means you set goals for yourself and do your utmost to fulfill them. Once one goal marker or mile post has been met, you move on to the next.

At its absolute simplest, Right Effort/Resolve is defined as:

Being resolved on renunciation, on freedom from ill will, on harmlessness.

(Majjhima Nikaya III.248)

So meditation isn't just about sitting still. It requires effort, will, and energy to monitor unwholesome thoughts and strive to eliminate them. If sitting still and being quiet were enough to end suffering, there would be no need to meditate. Thanks to the invention of television, billions do just that every day.

2. Right Mindfulness

The Sacca-Vibhanga Sutta also defines this clearly:

> *Here the monk remains contemplating the body as body, resolute, aware and mindful, having put aside worldly desire and sadness;*
>
> *he remains contemplating feelings as feelings;*
>
> *he remains contemplating mental states as mental states;*
>
> *he remains contemplating mental objects as mental objects, resolute, aware and mindful, having put aside worldly desire and sadness.*

This, then, is what mindfulness and meditation is all about. It is not running away from thoughts and feelings, nor attempting to suppress them. It simply doesn't work. Suppress one thought, and a million others will take its place. Suppress one feeling, and you increase its power ten-fold. If I ask you not to think about green monkeys, you cannot help but think about green monkeys. If I ask you not to be angry about something, you'll just become angrier.

Right Mindfulness is about watching your thoughts and feelings vigilantly – but to take a step back and not participate in them. Perhaps you can't help thinking about an argument you had with a friend. So remember the incident, but stop with the input. Often, when we remember an unpleasant encounter, we recreate it in our heads with a twist. We re-imagine the things we should have said and done and weave it into our memories to create the ideal scenario that would make us feel better.

This goes against Right Mindfulness which states that we should contemplate our feelings as feelings and mental states as mental states. In other words, we must take a passive approach by simply watching our thoughts and feelings instead of engaging them. Keep recreating the ideal scenario in your head and you feed the flames of your attachment.

You tell yourself, "Well I should have said this," or "I should have done that." The incident is over, it happened in the past. Adding commentary only fans the flames and brings the past to the present. The moment you start participating in those feelings and mental states instead of simply contemplating them, you cease to be in the present moment. You have instead dived back into the drama that's going on in your head – the drama that is causing you *dukkha*.

3. Right Concentration

The Sanskrit word for concentration is *samadhi* which can also mean clearness or a heightened state of mental alertness. This, too, the Sacca-Vibhanga Sutta explains in some detail:

> *Here, the monk, detached from sense-desires, detached from unwholesome states, enters and remains in the first level of concentration in which there is applied and sustained thinking, together with joy and pleasure born of detachment;*
> *And through the subsiding of applied and sustained thinking, with the gaining of inner stillness and oneness of mind, he enters and remains in the second level, which is without applied and sustained thinking, and in which there are joy and pleasure born of concentration;*
> *And through the fading of joy, he remains equanimous, mindful and aware, and he experiences in his body the pleasure of which the Noble Ones say: "equanimous, mindful and dwelling in pleasure", and thus he enters and remains in the third level;*
> *And through the giving up of pleasure and pain, and through the previous disappearance of happiness and sadness, he enters and remains in the fourth level, which is without pleasure and pain, and in which there is pure equanimity and mindfulness.*

So there are levels to Right Concentration. One leads to another if one patiently and diligently works toward one marker stone. Doing so leads one to the next, and so forth until one reaches that stage wherein pleasure and pain, sorrow and sadness no longer have the ability to shake one's inner mind.

Please note: This doesn't mean that one who achieves this state is incapable of feeling. Far from it. What the scripture refers to is a state of mind which is steady and no longer dependent on external factors to exist in the default state – that of tranquility. In this state, there is the joy of being self-sufficient in the emotional sense. A person who reaches this fourth level can still appreciate beauty, can still love, can still experience pleasure, and can still know happiness.

But they no longer become the victims of an emotional roller coaster ride that lets them be happy when beauty is present and sad when it fades or goes away. They can still feel love regardless of what the other person feels about them, can still experience pleasure regardless of their material circumstances, and can abide in happiness even when things change or pass away. Because though they still participate in the drama of life, they are able to stand back from it. In standing back, they are able to participate in the play and experience all of the exciting drama it has to offer with the same ease by which they can sit in the audience watching that play unfold.

**

That takes care of the theory. With the theory behind us, we now at last come to the actual practice of meditation, itself. There are many different forms of meditation practice available to Buddhists – so much so that vast libraries exist on the subject matter. In this book, we will focus on Calm Abiding and Insight.

Calm Abiding

The idea behind *Calm Abiding* meditation is that your mind is like a pool of water. In the beginning, the water is very disturbed. There are all sorts of ripples and waves on the surface. The mud at the bottom has been stirred up, and the water's now turbid, brown, and dirty. You can't see through it at all.

Calm abiding is about letting the water settle down, not disturbing it. As you leave the water alone, the waves subside. The surface becomes flat, calm, and reflective. The mud settles to the bottom of the pool, so the water becomes clear. So before you can use insight meditation to examine your mind and phenomena, it's important to work on Calm Abiding first, so that the mind naturally settles down and becomes clear and reflective.

Calm abiding meditation is not just a process of stilling the mind, but also of cultivating sustained attention. You could call this concentration, but it's not quite as strained as concentration. Instead, the kind of attention we're aiming for is steady and relaxed.

Cultivating the capacity for steady, relaxed attention is absolutely critical to Buddhist meditation. Attention is the instrument, like a microscope, through which we view the mind in meditation. So making sure we have a good capacity for attention is indispensable.

How to sit

It's traditional to sit cross-legged on a carpet or cushion. But if you have any kind of problem — such as a knee injury or chronic back pain — it's okay to sit on a chair. The most important point is to keep the spine straight. If you slouch, you will find it hard to maintain your attention, and the mind will go wandering or become drowsy.

- Traditionally, there are two ways to sit. The first is the way the Japanese do it – kneeling on a cushion that raises them some two or three inches above the floor with their knees pointing straight forward. The advantage of this position is that it forces one to sit up straight without placing any strain on the lower back. The problem with this position is the weight it brings to the legs and knees. Those who've not been sitting this way all their lives might find it uncomfortable to sustain over a long period.

  The other way to sit is in lotus position with your legs crossed in front of you – also called the Indian style. Although this posture is easier to maintain over a longer period, it also makes it easier to slouch.

  While many people in Asian cultures are used to sitting this way and can maintain such a position for long periods, those in the West who are more used to sitting on chairs might find it difficult to sustain for long.

  If you would prefer to sit on a chair, that's fine so long as you pick one that has no backrest. Your need to constantly maintain an upright posture is essential, because not only does it help to keep you awake, it also ensures that you maintain an upright posture. Sitting on a chair with a backrest brings on the temptation to slouch or to lean back which could affect your breathing.

- Your spine should be slightly arched so that your chest sticks out a little. This ensures that the weight of your chest and shoulders rests on the space between your shoulder blades. If you can't imagine this, clasp your hands behind your back. Now arch your back so you're looking up at the ceiling. Feel the strain between your shoulder blades? That's where the weight of your chest and shoulders should rest, but it requires you to keep your back arched a little. This is the best way to maintain an upright posture that's relaxed and causes no strain on your spine, whatsoever.

- Rest your hands face up on your lap near your knees. Doing so helps you maintain your balance, rolls your shoulders back, and opens up your chest cavity – the ideal posture for optimal breathing. An alternative is to place your palms above your groin, such that your right hand rests over your left hand. The fingers of your right hand should be pointing to the left side of your body, while the fingers of the left hand below pointed toward the right. Experiment to see which posture is most comfortable for you and that you feel you can maintain without effort.

- Your lips should remain together, but your jaw should be relaxed enough that there's a slight gap between your upper and lower teeth. Gently rest the tip of your tongue against the back of your upper teeth to minimize saliva production, and therefore, the need to constantly swallow – a major source of distraction.

- Keep your eyelids half closed and find a spot a few feet in front of you on the floor. Since you'll be staring down, find a position your eyes can maintain without any strain, whatsoever. During this meditation, you will not focus on anything. Whatever spot you choose on the floor is simply where your gaze will rest. Alternatively, you can close your eyes.

Mindfulness of the breath

Traditionally, a beginner in Calm Abiding starts with meditating on the breath. There is no fancy technique here, no special kind of breathing to do. In fact, you don't alter the breath at all. You just let it happen naturally and pay attention to the sensation of the breath in the nostrils, to the rise and fall of your chest, whether the breath is long or short, shallow or deep, slow or fast.

This process is called *mindfulness of the breath*. Mindfulness in meditation means that your mind is placed on an object, in this case the breath, and rests there without wavering. It sounds easy, but it's kind of tricky, because, as you'll discover, the mind is pretty wild and undisciplined. It's always getting distracted, wanders off, becomes unclear and drowsy, daydreams, fantasizes, suddenly becomes emotional, thinks about this and that — basically anything except being *mindful*.

In fact, if you've done a little meditation practice, you might have come to the conclusion that meditation has made your mind *worse*, that your mind is even more distracted, disturbed, and chaotic than it was before.

But the truth is that meditation doesn't make your mind more chaotic. It just makes you aware of how wild your mind has always been. Sometimes you'll hear meditation teachers refer to this as the "monkey mind." Monkeys rarely sit still. They are always jumping from branch to branch, scratching themselves, grooming other monkeys, fighting, trying to steal food, and looking here and there with sharp little eyes.

The untrained mind keeps a constant running commentary of discursive thought, except when it exhausts itself, in which case it just slips into a stupor. It's just like a monkey with its constant need for stimulation and activity.

The Calm Abiding approach to this distraction is just to let it go and return the mind to the breath. There's nothing wrong with getting distracted. In the context of meditation, the thoughts that you have are not good or bad. It doesn't matter if your thoughts are greedy or charitable, hateful or compassionate, nice or mean. If any kind of thoughts or feelings come up, label them "thinking." Then drop them and return to the breath.

It's very important not to get discouraged or reproach yourself for getting distracted. Sometimes you sit down to meditate, and from the moment you land on the cushion until it's time to get up, your mind scarcely stays on the breath for a single second. That's okay and need not be regarded as a problem.

One of the things we're trying to give up in meditation is this judgmental mind that wants to categorize everything as good and bad and push its own agenda.

Meditation is about not having an agenda. Mindfulness is not some new agenda that you force on yourself. Instead, it's about carving out a piece of time to just rest, what Chögyam Trungpa (a Tibetan Buddhist monk and author) called "virgin time" in which you just sit and do nothing.

Sitting there, just paying attention to the breath, is very close to doing nothing at all. In fact, the next stage of Calm Abiding from mindfulness of the breath is called objectless meditation, where you just sit and don't pay attention to anything at all. You just let the mind rest completely, without an object, but still aware and alert and undistracted. So mindfulness of the breath is, in some sense, like a preparation for doing nothing.

In the beginning you might find it helpful to count the breath. So as you breathe in, then out — that's one. Again breathe in, and out — two. And so on up to ten. Once you reach ten, start again from one. If you get distracted, then just start over again from one. It also helps to start with short sessions of just five or ten minutes, and gradually sit for longer periods.

After some time, you might reach the point in your practice where you find counting the breath to be too heavy-handed. At this point, it's not necessary to keep counting. Just drop the counting altogether and place your mind on the breath itself, paying attention to its sensations and qualities.

Watchfulness

Mindfulness is resting the mind on the breath and keeping it there. It is about an even, sustained attention to an object. When distraction happens, the mind gets preoccupied and forgets its object. It goes off somewhere, maybe on a trip to the beach. Or it replays a scene from work, or makes plans for later. Whatever it may be, it doesn't matter.

At some point you catch yourself wandering and remember to return the mind to the breath. That's called *watchfulness* or awareness. Watchfulness catches deviations from the object and corrects them. It also catches you if you slide into either the extreme of excitement or dullness. Over time, watchfulness will naturally get better and better at what it does. It will catch deviations more quickly and return to the object more smoothly. Mindfulness and watchfulness work together, with mindfulness keeping the mind on the breath and watchfulness returning it to the breath when it goes somewhere else.

Insight Meditation

A regular practice of Calm Abiding makes your mind peaceful, spacious, attentive, and workable. It can give you a powerful sense of centeredness and well-being. A wealth of scientific research shows that mindfulness meditation, a subset of Calm Abiding, is very effective at treating common emotional problems such as stress, anxiety, and depression. It will help you regulate your emotions and give you an overall positive outlook on life that is natural, not forced.

So even if you limit yourself to just this kind of meditation, there are tremendous benefits. But from the point of view of Buddhism, the path of meditation doesn't end with Calm Abiding. That's just one milestone on the road.

Calm Abiding is intended to lay the groundwork for Insight Meditation, or *vipassana*. Remember how we compared Calm Abiding to a microscope? Well, Insight Meditation is about actually aiming that microscope at your own mind, your own experience, to get to the bottom of its nature. By getting to the bottom of things, you undo the original ignorance that causes you to cycle through the same feedback loop again and again, generating further and further states of *dukkha*.

This is where all the legwork of understanding the theory from the first chapter will really pay off. First you ground yourself in some general understanding of your predicament as an individual who experiences *dukkha*. Then you set the mood by practicing the ethics of non-harm. Then you make the mind and attention powerful, flexible, and clear through the practice of Calm Abiding. Then you're ready to start untangling the big knotted mass of neurotic mind through Insight Meditation practice.

This is why the Eightfold Path is not to be viewed as some sort of grocery list that you go through one by one. It must rather be understood as the different sections of a single movement with one goal. The steps provided in Calm Abiding – from the proper way to sit, to the proper way to hold your hands, and so forth – are an excellent way to understand the entirety of the Eightfold Path.

Some modern courses teach Insight Meditation from the very beginning. I'm not knocking that approach, but I do think the Buddha had good reasons for prescribing a foundation of Calm Abiding before starting to do Insight Meditation. One reason is that, if your mind is not very calm and stable already because of Calm Abiding practice, your practice of Insight Meditation will be unstable, and you will be prone to emotional disturbances. It's a pretty intense practice.

Specifically, you traditionally cultivate certain states called *jhanas* before starting insight meditation. The *jhanas* are progressive states of subtler and subtler meditative levels of awareness as described in the Sacca-Vibhanga Sutta. First you master one, then proceed to the next. The Buddha learned how to practice the *jhanas* from his teachers. They were cutting edge high-level mental technology, but he felt that he still hadn't achieved what he wanted from his search. He wanted to go beyond this level.

Insight Meditation is how you do that. The idea is, you've already mastered these extremely subtle meditative states. Then you enter into them and, from this very subtle and calm state, start examining all the elements of experience and your mind. You look at the phenomena of your mind as well as external phenomena. And you find, again and again, that they have three characteristic properties:

1. They are impermanent.
2. They are unsatisfactory (*dukkha*).
3. They are not the self.

When Buddhism talks about impermanence, it means that, at the most subtle level of understanding, nothing remains the same even for a moment. In fact, all conditioned phenomena arise, abide, and cease in a single moment.

So take, for example, your computer, tablet, or Kindle — whatever you're using to read this book. It *seems* to be a solid, continuously existing thing. Not only that, but it appears to be a *single* thing — that is, you probably experience it as a one object, one device. But, in fact, it is not a single thing. It is made up of a number of parts which can be separated. If you accidentally drop it on the ground, you may suddenly find out just how not single it is. I'm sure we've all had similar run-ins with impermanence.

Just as it seems to be one single object but is, in reality, not, so it also seems to be one continuous object that exists over time — but it isn't. It consists of a series of moments in constant flux. Each moment is like a single frame in a film reel. When you're watching the film, the frames follow one another so quickly that your mind is fooled into thinking they're all one continuous scene. That's just how our perception is set up.

But if you slow that film reel down, you will notice that each frame is a discrete and separate thing, and the movement and continuity you perceived before were just an illusion. Through a continuous and sustained practice of Insight Meditation, your mind begins to change. It becomes slow, precise, and accurate – a process that begins first with Calm Abiding. Then, when you aim it at phenomena — both your own mind and the external world — you find that seemingly continuous phenomena is actually constantly flickering in an out of existence. And that's when, for you, the illusion of permanence is broken.

If that sounds trippy and intense, it is. But that's not everything. When you aim that meditative mind at yourself — at your five aggregates of form, feeling, perception, conditioning, and consciousness — you find that they are also made of many parts that are constantly flickering in and out of existence.

What once seemed a single person existing continuously in time — that is, *you* — turns out to be just a kaleidoscopic stream of constantly shifting and changing events, flickering in and out, with no single essence holding them all together. That's the experience of non-self. This is what Buddhism means when it says that the self is just an illusion that comes about from our habits of thought.

Because both your person and your environment have no ultimate permanence or stability, they are ultimately unsatisfactory – *dukkha*. We cling to these things as real, solid, continuous, permanent, because their actual impermanence freaks us out. But this is a mistake, because the self and sense objects are like sand castles. The next tide will wash them away.

Chapter 5: Schools of Buddhism

At the beginning of this book, I said that the aim is not to convert you to Buddhism but to talk about Buddhism as a practical philosophy of life. That's still the case, but you might be wondering about Buddhism's more traditional manifestations. Or maybe you've followed the program a bit, but you want to take the next step and learn from a teacher or join a community of like-minded people. Then again, maybe you're just curious and want to follow up with more resources. If so, then this chapter is for you.

Following the Buddha's death, his followers carried on the tradition of his teachings in India for centuries. Buddhism also proved to be India's most popular export of all time, more so than even yoga. It spread all throughout Asia, from Iran in the west to Japan in the east, from parts of Siberia in the north all the way to Sri Lanka, Indonesia, and the Maldives in the south. The Buddhist emperor Ashoka even sent a mission of monks to Alexandria in Egypt to teach the Dharma to the Greeks. These monks probably followed the Theravada, as they gave rise to a tradition of hermits in Egypt called *Therapeutae,* from which we get our word "therapy." These Therapeutae were the inspiration for the later Christian tradition of meditation and monasticism.

As Buddhism grew and spread, it developed into different schools. Eventually two major schools emerged: the Theravada and the Mahayana. Then, around the seventh century, another school became very popular it Tibet. Only in recent years did it spread far and wide. That school is called the Vajrayana or Tibetan Buddhism.

1. Theravada

Theravada Buddhism, also known as southern Buddhism, is most widespread in Southeast Asian countries — Thailand, Burma, Cambodia, Laos, Vietnam, and Sri Lanka, as well as parts of India, Bangladesh, and China. It has over 100 million followers worldwide. Theravada translates into English as "school of the elder monks," or as lay Buddhists say, "the old school."

The Theravada claim to follow the original teachings of the Buddha faithfully. All of the quoted scriptures in the earlier chapters of this book come from Theravada texts. That's because they serve as the baseline that most schools of Buddhism accept as the fundamental teachings of the Buddha, the entry-point for Mahayana and Vajrayana.

The Theravada teachings center around the Four Noble Truths and the noble Eightfold Path. In a nutshell, the Four Noble Truths are:

1. Life is *dukkha*.
2. The cause of *dukkha* is ignorance and neurosis.
3. It's possible to bring an end to *dukkha*.
4. *Dukkha* can be ended by following the noble Eightfold Path.

The noble Eightfold Path can also be summed up in three parts: worldview, lifestyle, and meditation. We already went over these points at length. The Theravada path culminates in becoming an *arahant* (or *arhat*) – someone who has completely eliminated suffering and the view of the self, thereby attaining *nirvana* in Sanskrit, or *nibbana* in Pali (the language the Buddha taught in).

Nirvana/nibbana is the cessation of suffering. Some believe that the etymology comes from the Sanskrit words *nir* (meaning no, none, without) and *vana* (meaning forest). The idea here is that the forest surrounds us on all sides, cutting off our clear view of where we are and what the world is like. When the forest is gone, we can see clearly in all directions. Not all linguists agree with this interpretation, but it is one that is often used in many Theravada schools to help give people an idea of what *nirvana/nibbana* is like.

The core institution of the Theravada tradition is the Sangha or assembly of monks and nuns, though it also refers to the lay Buddhist community at large. In fact, Theravada has become quite popular in the West in recent years, and has inspired the Insight Meditation or *vipassana* movement.

The modern Insight Meditation movement teaches techniques that involve scanning your body and mind for sensations and feelings. You notice how every element of your experience has the three marks of existence: impermanence, *dukkha*, and non-self. This trains your mind to have deeper and deeper insights into how these truths play out in your own experience. Eventually, the process culminates in realization and, finally, liberation from *dukkha* and the self-destructive feedback loop.

Many modern people in the West have found the Theravada teachings extremely valuable and helpful in their lives – especially since it places less emphasis on ritual and more on meditative practice. Through intensive meditation retreats, they've made personal discoveries through Insight Meditation and found within it something more profound than a form of stress relief or a vacation from their daily lives. They've found a practice that gives them a deeper understanding of how suffering, dissatisfaction, and negativity arise. It gives them a guide to navigating these difficulties and living their lives gently and nobly.

2. Mahayana

In Theravada the goal of the path is arhatship – the stage where one dwells in *nirvana*. But Mahayanists see complete buddhahood as the ultimate goal of the path. According to Mahayana, the path of the arhat is a valid but lower path which focuses on one's individual liberation.

In contrast to this, Mahayana upholds the ideal of universal liberation. Mahayana means "the great vehicle." The idea is of a ship that crosses the stormy ocean of existence called *samsara* and reaches the shore of *nirvana*. The ship is "great" because it carries all beings in it instead of just one.

So the hero of Mahayana Buddhism is the bodhisattva, or saint. A bodhisattva is a practitioner that has vowed to walk the spiritual path not for him or herself alone, but in order to liberate all beings and bring them into enlightenment or awakening. Some bodhisattvas vow not to become a buddha until they can first liberate every other being. Others aim to become a buddha first, and then bring others into enlightenment.

The aspiration to put others first and lift them up out of the feedback loop of *samsara* is called *bodhicitta*, the intention of enlightenment. Bodhisattvas do this because of their deep compassion for all beings that suffer from neurosis, ignorance, and pain. They are deeply moved by the suffering of others and want to remove it by the root. That means uprooting passion, aggression, confusion, and their causes – fundamental ignorance.

Mahayanists also believe in something called *emptiness*. Emptiness takes the idea of non-self and carries it a step further. Not only do the five aggregates lack a singular, independent essence that we could label "myself," but all things lack any inner independent core. According to Mahayana, phenomena exists only in as much as they're related to each other and to the minds of the beings that perceive them. In other words, all beings participate in the unfolding of phenomenon.

So for Mahayanists, the world is dream-like and insubstantial. It is like an illusion that brings us under its spell and seduces us into an endless sleep of neurosis and confusion. When this illusion evaporates, all that is left is the bright inner radiance of the luminous mind we talked about earlier. This luminous mind is what Mahayana calls the *Buddha nature*.

Buddha nature doesn't come into existence because of meditating and walking the path. It's there from the very beginning, waiting to be discovered. Every being has Buddha nature. It is because we have Buddha nature that we have the chance to become a buddha. To become a buddha, you have to remove the many layers of neurosis and habitual patterns that keep you trapped in the illusion.

It's as if there were a pure, perfect mirror. But it can't reflect anything because it's covered in many centuries of dirt and grime. From that perspective, the point of the Mahayana path is to take a cloth and scrub and scrub and scrub the mirror clean. Slowly you get rid of the dirt and grime. When the mirror is clean again, you can reflect your bright light to others, which inspires them to clean their own mirrors and discover their innate Buddha nature.

Mahayana is generally divided into two basic schools best explained through the following two poems:

> *This body is the tree of enlightenment*
> *The mind is like a mirror bright.*
> *Take heed to keep it always clean,*
> *And let no dust collect upon it.*
> (Shen Xiu)

The reply was:

> *Enlightenment is not like a tree.*
> *The mirror bright is nowhere shining.*
> *As there is nothing from the first,*
> *Where does the dust itself collect?*
> (Hui Neng)

They contradict each other because Shen Xiu (a Chinese Buddhist monk) came from the northern Mahayana School which teaches that there is an Ultimate Reality which can be achieved through hard work, meditation, and study – resulting in *nirvana*. Hui Neng, on the other hand, came from the Southern School which teaches that there's no such thing as a tree or a mirror with an independent existence. It's only a mirror or a tree because we say it is.

The other thing that distinguishes Mahayana is its acceptance of scriptures other than the Pali scriptures directly attributed to the historical Buddha. They also accept a myriad of gods, goddesses, and other supernatural beings in their daily devotions.

Theravadan Buddhists generally do not. In the first chapter, the picture of Budai was presented in order to compare it to traditional depictions of Siddhartha Gautama – the historical Buddha. Budai was a Chinese Buddhist monk who lived in 900 AD and was believed by Chinese Mahayanists to have achieved Buddhahood. Such acceptance of a vast pantheon of saints is another practice which differentiates Mahayana from Theravada.

Today the Mahayana is followed in Tibet, China, Japan, Korea, Vietnam, Mongolia, and parts of Russia, as well as Indonesia.

Zen

Zen is perhaps the most famous Mahayana school. It has become a household name and needs no introduction. The word "zen" conjures images of austerity and discipline, but also peace, simplicity, and beauty.

Zen Buddhism enters history with Bodhidharma, a Persian monk and "blue-eyed barbarian" who showed up mysteriously in China around the 5th or 6th century (accounts vary). He claimed to be 150 years old and is depicted as a scowling, bearded figure with Central Asian features.

Zen Buddhism was called *Chan* in China, which is probably a Chinese pronunciation of the Sanskrit *dhyan*, meaning meditation. Bodhidharma taught a very direct, meditation-focused form of teaching that involved a lot of discipline and focus. His teaching was very simple: still the mind, look within, and see your own Buddha nature directly.

Zen practitioners like Hui Neng believe that knowledge can come from a direct, wordless transmission of wisdom — "a special transmission outside of the scriptures." They claim that this knowledge began when the Buddha transmitted his insight to his disciple Mahakashyapa by silently showing him a flower. Mahākāśyapa was enlightened through this gesture, so the Buddha allegedly said:

"I possess the true Dharma eye, the marvelous mind of Nirvāna, the true form of the formless, the subtle Dharma gate that does not rest on words or letters but is a special transmission outside of the scriptures. This I entrust to Mahākāśyapa."

Based on this myth, Zen emphasizes meditation and the passing of insight from teacher to disciple. It places practice and experience over scholarship, though it venerates many esteemed historical figures.

Zen flourished in China and spread to other parts of East Asia: Japan, Korea, and Vietnam. Today there are two main schools of Zen in Japan – Soto and Rinzai. Soto emphasizes "just sitting" as its main meditation practice, while Rinzai emphasizes meditation on puzzling aphorisms, riddles, or pieces of dialogue called *koans*.

Koans include such questions as "What is your original face before you were born?" The student contemplates these riddles as a means of breaking the ordinary concepts of the ignorant, discursive mind and see the truth beyond concepts. Koans often arise out of teaching situations. For example:

A monk asked Master Haryo, "What is the way?"

Haryo said, "An open-eyed man falling into the well."

The idea here is that meditation is an exploration into the unknown nature of one's self. Unless and until one follows it, they cannot possibly know where it will lead. They can read books and listen to what others have to say about it, but until they fall into it, they cannot truly know.

Like Theravada, Zen has proven very popular in the West, even becoming an oft-referenced (and misunderstood) item in pop culture. But it's an extraordinary and profound tradition that appeals to people who want to follow a path that's direct, powerful, and not overly analytical.

Pure Land

The Pure Land school developed in China and is based on a genre of Mahayana scriptures that deal with celestial regions called pure lands or Buddha fields. In Mahayana cosmology, these pure lands emanated from the minds of various buddhas. They are places where people can travel the path to enlightenment quickly and easily without worldly distractions and sufferings. A Buddha field is not quite like the concept of heaven. It's not the final destination. It's more like a halfway house to enlightenment.

The Pure Land School was founded by Huiyuan in 402 AD. Followers of Pure Land develop faith and devotion for Amitabha or "Infinite Light," a celestial buddha who reigns over a pure land called Sukhavati, "The Blissful." Practitioners repeatedly chant the name of Amitabha hoping to reach Amitabha's pure land after death.

Other practices in Pure Land Buddhism involve chanting a *dharani* or long mantra of Amitabha's pure land, as well as meditative visualizations of Buddha Amitabha and his circle of bodhisattvas in their pure land.

Here, the stress is on devotion, faith, and rituals – not meditation. The simplicity of the practice is what makes it very accessible to people from all walks of life. As such, it has been enormously popular with laypeople.

Pure Land has an established presence in the West, but it has not achieved nearly as much popularity as Zen, Theravada, and Tibetan Buddhism.

3. Vajrayana

The Vajrayana or "Adamantine Vehicle" is part of Mahayana but also constitutes its own distinct system. Vajrayana is also known as Tantric Buddhism.

Though once more widely practiced throughout parts of Asia, only three traditions survive today in Japan (called *Shingon*), Nepal, and Tibet.

Of these three, the Tibetan Vajrayana is the most popular today because of the Dalai Lama. Tibetan Buddhism is practiced in Tibet, Mongolia, parts of Siberia, and the Russian Federal state of Kalmykia.

Tibetan Vajrayana is a mixture of Mahayana Buddhism, Hinduism, and Bon – the original religion of Tibet which still survives today. It is a philosophy, a religion, as well as the original political system of Tibet before the Chinese takeover. In other words, it is a theocratic system with the Dalay Lama as its priest-king.

Vajrayana accepts the Mahayana program of the bodhisattva path of compassion and the goal of complete buddhahood. What makes it unique is a huge collection of special practices and rituals that are said to constitute special methods for attaining the goals of the Mahayana much faster.

According to Vajrayana, both the Theravada and Mahayana are "causal vehicles." That is, they rely on building up the causes for enlightenment over a long period of time. That's a fine approach, according to Vajrayana, but it takes a very, very long time.

Vajrayana, on the other hand, starts by assuming the end goal has already been reached. Enlightenment or buddhahood is already full and complete within the practitioner. So instead of the practitioner trying to dig down through all the layers to reach Buddha nature, in Vajrayana, the Buddha nature digs itself out. It dissolves through the layers of conceptuality and neurosis from within.

Vajrayana is about transformation. One kind of transformation has to do with perception. According to Vajrayana, confused beings perceive the world as impure and full of suffering and negativity. Vajrayana's approach is to transform impure perception into pure perception through special practices which destroy the impediments that keep us stuck in the feedback loop of suffering. But Vajrayana does not advocate rejecting passion, aggression, and confusion. It teaches that the innermost nature of these negative phenomena is pure wisdom.

The metaphor that's used is of a tree with poisonous fruit. The approach of Theravada is to cut the tree down. Mahayana advocates pulling the tree up from its roots. The approach of Vajrayana is to take the poison and use it to make medicine.

Therefore, the Vajrayana doesn't reject anything. Desire, anger, sexuality — everything is fuel for the path. Every kind of experience, good or bad, is fundamentally good in the Vajrayana and can be brought onto the spiritual path. Even the most apparently negative aspects of our lives are rich and full of energy. They are a colorful palette which we can use to paint our canvas.

The Vajrayana path begins with an initiation called empowerment. Empowerment is given by a lama or guru and brings the student into the mandala of whichever system they will be practicing. Once in the mandala, the student has the blessings and permission they need to perform Vajrayana practices.

Empowerment can only be given by a qualified guru. Because the practices are said to be dangerous and can lead to very serious consequences if people take them the wrong way, students need to practice them under the guidance of a qualified spiritual teacher who can steer them away from the pitfalls and hazards of the path.

Conclusion

The main message of Buddhism is that real freedom from the neurotic mind, real freedom from *dukkha*, is possible by digging up ignorance by its root and cultivating the direct experience of non-self. It may sound a little scary to do so, but it shouldn't be, because beyond our self-protective habits of mind is a pure and free state of being that cannot be created or destroyed.

This state of being has been compared to the vast reaches of space. Space is empty and void, but it is also infinite and deathless. It accommodates everything whatsoever within its expanse. It has nothing to gain or lose, nothing to hope for, and nothing to fear. It gives no reference points, offers nothing to grasp on to. It is complete and sufficient unto itself.

This ultimate state of utter purity is *nirvana*, the final fruit of the Buddhist path, but we don't have to rely on a distant promise of it. It can be glimpsed in a partial way, like a reflection, right now, through the practice of meditation.

Nirvana isn't heaven. It isn't a place out there to be achieved upon death, nor a reward for good behavior. It is a state of mind that can be attained in the here and now – the reward for consistent and determined effort in applying the Eightfold Path.

There are times in meditative practice when the dense thicket of discursive thought suddenly falls away, when the games and self-deceptions of ego-clinging subside. It is as if the sky had been covered by clouds, but suddenly they parted and revealed the vast blue sky. Then you're left with an experience of the luminous mind:

Luminous, monks, is the mind. And it is freed from incoming defilements. The well-instructed disciple of the noble ones discerns that as it actually is present, which is why I tell you that—for the well-instructed disciple of the noble ones—there is development of the mind.

(Pabhassara Sutta)

The luminous mind lies behind the veils of neurotic mind. Getting a taste or a glimpse of it is, as the Buddha says in the quote above, the condition for walking the path and developing the mind through meditation.

This is not some distant hope, a dream deferred until the next life, but an immanent reality that could be experienced right now. It is waiting for anyone fortunate and bold enough to try.

Are you?

Made in the USA
Monee, IL
05 May 2022

95936496R10046